WHEN HOPE IS NOT ENOUGH

Ahmed Miqdad

Cover Photograph by Khaled El Sabah

Other titles by Ahmed Miqdad

Gaza Narrates Poetry
available on Amazon and Kindle

PREFACE

It is a worthwhile duty to write about Palestine and express our love and patriotism through words. Palestine is the heart that enriches us with strength and ability, it is the womb that carries us and nourishes us through sacrifice and freedom. Palestine is the compassionate mother who takes care of her children.

I wrote my poems to make our voice so loud that the whole world will hear the pain and suffering of Palestine.

The suffering of the Palestinians began in1948, when the Israelis occupied the Palestinian lands, killed the innocent, obliged families to evacuate from their villages and homes and forced them to emigrate to other villages and cities. The Israeli occupation didn't stop there: the Israelis then started committing atrocities and war crimes against the Palestinian refugees in Lebanon and killed the Palestinians in the cities of Palestine. They cut down the trees and demolished homes to make Palestine seem like a land without people and to try to deceive the whole world with this lie. They tried to erase the Arabic and Islamic history from the books, libraries and streets in an attempt to persuade the world that this land is Israeli, not Palestinian.

Gaza is one of the cities to which our parents were obliged to emigrate after1948. They settled and waited for years in the hope of returning to their villages - but that hope was in vain.

Gaza is the chief witness of the Israeli crimes not only against the Palestinians but against humanity. Many wars have happened during a short period of time. These wars were launched by the Israelis against the Palestinians in Gaza city. As a result of the wars, thousands of Palestinians were killed; there have been thousands of wounded, many orphans, a vast number of widows, and a multitude of homes destroyed. Palestinians lost their beloved children, fathers, mothers and relatives, so you can find in each Palestinian home in Gaza a martyr, a wounded person, a prisoner or an orphan who lost his or her parents because of the Israeli bombs dropped on Gaza. The streets of Gaza bear witness to the Israeli war crimes: the smell of blood and decay blowing through the streets becomes a wind of inspiration which urges us to paint this picture and show it to the world through words, because they are the only weapon we have as writers in Palestine.

I wrote my book through the hardest conditions we have ever witnessed since I was born. I wrote my first book,Gaza Narrates Poetry, during the days of the last war on Gaza, which lasted fifty-one days. This, my second book, was written after the war. I tried to present the reader with the knowledge and images of Gaza through my poems as clearly as I possibly could. I wrote many poems about the conditions of life in Gaza under eight years of siege; these poems describe the suffering and pain of the families, especially the orphans and widows,who lost their children and relatives, and express my feelings towards my beloved homeland Palestine, which I will never cease to love.

I would like to tell you that I wrote my second book despite the crisis conditions in Gaza: power which comes on for just six hours a day, oppression, depression, terror, sad feelings, and Gaza's damaged economy. I did my best to make this book accessible to my readers, activists and supporters worldwide. I hope I have succeeded in painting an exact picture of real life in Gaza to show the world what has been happening during and after the Israeli wars on Gaza. I tried to clarify the image of the ugly Israeli occupation that has no mercy on innocents, children, or the elderly. They even have no mercy on animals or trees. I want to expose the scandal of the Israeli atrocities and massacres committed upon my people here in Gaza.

I wrote my poems from the beating of my heart and the vision of my eyes straight to the readers' hearts and minds.

I hope you like my poems and understand the messages in them. Then you can show your support as a human being to the Palestinian cause. I hope the reader will have a positive experience reading this book of poems that describes the suffering of innocent people in Gaza. Please spread the word about this book, and encourage your friends to read it.

DEDICATION

I dedicate my book to:

Palestine,

The souls of martyrs,

The widows and orphans,

The suffering and pain of the wounded,

The Palestinian prisoners inside the Israeli jails,

All activists and supporters worldwide,

All seekers of freedom and justice,

My lovely parents and family,

My friends and relatives.

CONTENTS

Preface   i

Acknowledgments

Dedication

1   A Colorful Dress   1

2   A Story of Lovers   3

3   Compulsory Immigration   7

4   Dignity Is Our Identity   11

5   Gaza… Just Four Letters   15

6   It Will Never Be Broken   17

7   Some Glasses Of Whiskey   19

8   How Can I Forget You?   21

9   Jerusalem   25

10   My Pride   27

11   My Son they Killed You   29

12   A Leg or a Heart?   31

CONTENTS....2

13	Please Don't Come	33
14	The Apartheid Wall Will Fall	35
15	Gaza The Big Prison	37
16	The key	41
17	A night of Autumn	43
18	The Red Pillow	45
19	The Robbers	47
20	The Sky of Gaza is Raining	49
21	Enas – The Young Martyr	53
22	Waiting for the Ship	55
23	We Will Smile	57
24	Gaza Will Stand UpAgain	59
25	Who Am I?!	61
26	Wounded Gaza	65
27	The Walking Dead	67

ACKNOWLEDGEMENTS

First of all, my deep thanks and praises to Almighty Allah, who gifted me with the ability to write poetry and be able to express my feelings through powerful words.

Second, my gratitude to Palestine, who carried me in her womb to be a Palestinian. Especially my city Gaza, which teaches me the meaning of patience and sacrifice.

Third, my prayers and dua'a to the martyrs who inspired me with their blood to write such thoughtful poems. In addition, my sincere wishes to all the wounded who inspired me with their suffering and pain to translate them into words and make the whole world hear your cries.

Fourth, I would like to thank all my friends who supported me to take the first step in my career as a writer. They encouraged me to write more poems and now I have accomplished my second book.

Fifth, infinite thanks to my close brothers and sisters like Hank Lawler, Magdalena Karandeniz, and Nisfa Majed. They never stop encouraging and supporting me to continue my writing.

Sixth, my special thanks to my dear friend and sister Sarah Strudwick a fellow author, who never complains, but helps me edit, format and publish my books with the kind co-operation of my sister Nisfa Majed.

Seventh, my gratefulness to my parents who never stop mentioning me in their prayers, especially my mother who has such a kind heart.

Eighth, I extend my eternal love to my special wife Amal, who always appreciates and encourages me to write more. And to the little angels, Dana, Kareem, and Yazan, who inspire me to write about the suffering of children in Gaza in the hope of bringing a beautiful future to them.

Ninth, my continuing thanks to my friends in the United Kingdom and the USA like Katherine, Selina, Marsha Louque and Esther Wheatley for agreeing to edit my poems and giving essential recommendations and suggestions.

Finally, I would like to thank all my family and Gazan friends who appreciate my work to convey the true picture of the Palestinians to the worldwide community. Especially Rami and Mohammed. In addition to that, I would like to thank everybody who has helped to make this book a reality.

A COLORFUL DRESS

Under that olive tree far away,
and as the morning appears,
and the sun sends its rays.

So many years ago,
and before the building of the ugly wall,
cut the hearts and lands apart,
an old lady with an old bag,
carries some cloth and cords,
she used to visit the farm every day,
sit under the old olive tree,
sew her new clothes,
she was wearing a Palestinian dress,
and she is going to make a new one,
she started with the red cord,
near the neck of the dress,
to represent the blood of the martyrs,
who sacrifice for Palestine.

Then she moved to another color,
it was the black one,
to represent the massacres and crimes,
committed by the Israelis,
and the black days Palestine passed,
such wars, racism, attacks,
killing, atrocities, and assassinations.

AHMED MIQDAD

The sun was going to sleep away,

she moved with her bag,
to return back tomorrow,
the day was so peaceful and beautiful,
under the olive tree,
she got out her cloth and cords,
with a very sharp needle,
she started to sew the dress,
the new color was green,
to show the green fields,
that represent olive trees and oranges,
in memory of the beautiful days,
which were full of freedom and happiness,
and to indicate to the ownership of the land.

Finally, she got out the white color,
to fill the empty area of the dress,
she started filling,
with a big smile on her face,
I asked "Why this color particularly?",
she replied "This represents the pureness,
of Love, peace, and freedom".

The dress became so colorful,
it has a lot of meanings,
so beautiful and attractive,
it was so difficult to describe,
I wondered " Who are you?",
she replied " I am Palestine".

A STORY OF LOVERS

There in the narrow roads,
of our simple village,
near the valley and mountains,
the sky is so beautiful,
and during the night,
the moon monitors the darkness,
and witnesses our pure love,
we were sitting near the water,
telling each other our stories,
they were so pure,
we were just twelve.

Then war started,
destroyed our homes,
and demolished our hearts,
and our parents were killed,
no-one of us knows,
any news about the other.

Days of not knowing,
and no one takes care of me,
I moved to an orphanage,
I was alone there,
writes the messages to her,
and dreams every night of her,
asks Allah to keep her safe.

Hard years of waiting,
to see her again,

some years later,
she was brought to the orphanage,
with a pale face,
and sad heart for her loss,
of her mother and father,
we met each other happily,
and we started to draw the future,
to be her father , mother,
brother, friend and husband,
we became as one body,
which has two souls.

Now we are engaged,
and we arranged to be married,
but what happened was unexpected,
the enemy arrested me,
in a demonstration of the land day,
and the judge was stubborn,
he declared a severe sentence,
ten years of jail.

In that ugly and dark prison,
they separated us from each other,
every Monday there was a visit,
she used to bring clothes and money,
and her tears stand,
at the gates of her eyes,
they carry the bitterness of pain,
and the difficult life we face,
she sat down just fifteen minutes,
it is the allowed time.

Later we decided to break the barriers,
and get a baby of us,
I secretly gave her my sperm,

in a small tube,
during one of the visits.

After two visits,
she came with the smile,
that she is pregnant,
and some months later,
a lovely baby came with her,
he is my new born baby,
so hard to see the moment,
your child sees you,
inside the dark jail.

Year after year,
as he was getting older,
till the time is over,
and my freedom becomes real,
to live with my family,
and repeat the lovely days,
with my lover,
out of the prison gate.

AHMED MIQDAD

COMPULSORY IMMIGRATION

Since he was born,
he was like an orphan,
never having a father,
he was raised under the care of his mother,
with four brothers.

The father was killed by the Israeli gangs,
their mother was both parents,
he was five years old,
when the Israeli immigrants,
came to settle Palestine,
they forced the Palestinians,
to leave their homes and farms,
to leave their villages and cities,
keep Palestine empty,
to be ready for Israelis.

That young boy narrates,
the whole story all these years,
to all his grandsons,
he remembers all events,
when the Israeli gangs attacked the village,
he, his brothers and their mother,
left the home with some clothes,
after the killing and terrorism,
of the Israeli gangs against the Palestinians,
they left the village on feet,

AHMED MIQDAD

walked along the coast of Palestine,

during the compulsory immigration,
we were very hungry and thirsty,
my mother was so tired,
she carried some clothes,
we were crying because of hunger,
asked our mother for food,
but she carries nothing,
except our simple clothes,
she used to say, be patient.

When we reach there,
we will find food,
this continued till we reached Gaza,
we were so tired and weak,
then we stopped to take rest,
but there was no sign of food.

Suddenly, we looked there away,
there was a Bedouin with a cow,
he was coming from the pasture,
when he reached us,
the cow fell down,
the leg of the cow was broken,
he hit it to stand up,
but that was in vain,
then he brought his knife,
and slaughtered it,
he took some meat and asked us,
to take what we need from the cow,
our mother was so happy,
we had found food,
we ate until our stomachs were full.

And I advise you, my grandsons,

to be more patient and have faith,
because one day we will return,
if not me, you will.

AHMED MIQDAD

DIGNITY IS OUR IDENTITY

Souls are presented,
as gifts are taken,
blood paints the way,
to the walkers,
martyrs have gone there,
waiting the coming ones,
in the far heaven,
close to their Lord,
complain about the injustice,
homes are demolished,
by the rockets of the cowards,
throw bombs from planes,
kills parents, children,
young, or old,
they don't care.

Wounded are screaming,
because of the deep wounds,
no sleep or rest,
the pain replaces the comfort,
sleep is no friend,
destroys the future,
after losing some body parts,
of the burnt body.

Orphaned children are everywhere,
some lost their father,

some lost their mothers,

some lost both,
and some lost all the family.

Widows mourn their losses,
cry all through the night,
take care of the orphans,
draw their stories of misery,
gather the children together,
show them love and compassion,
fulfill their needs,
it is a hard and difficult life,
such Miserable conditions,
a lethal enemy,
but we teach life,
because dignity is our identity.
"First Eid To Your Farewell"
The mosques call Allah is The Greatest,
while I was saying,
Allah is The Greatest,
against the one who killed you.

Your farewell is so difficult,
our heart is wrenching in pain,
our family is missing you,
like the one who lost his limbs,
we used to live together,
share our sadness and happiness.

The Eid comes,
while you are far away,
why don't you come?!,
who took you away from us?!,

who made us sad for the rest of our lives?!,
who stole you from us?!.

You used to bring smiles,
our lips miss the laughter,
our faces tell of sad tales,
you used to bring sweets,
during preparation for Eid,
who will bring sweets this Eid?!,
who will buy clothes for the children?!,
who will bring toys to the children?!.

We will miss you,
as tears fill our eyes,
our hearts cry for you,
you were the light in our darkness,
the safety during our fear,
you are our happiness,
when sadness storms us.

how can we smile?!,
while your blood is still wet,
and our tears have not dried.

How can we feel joy?!,
your children ask about you,
who used to go with you,
and pray Eid's prayers,
who are unaware of your death,
they Ask about you,
when they said where is Papa?,
and I reply "he is there",
Awaiting us in paradise.

AHMED MIQDAD

How can we feel Eid?!,
when our homes are destroyed,

our clothes buried under the rubble,
And your son sits in a wheelchair.

How can we feel happy?!
people go to visit their relatives,
go to parks and restaurants,
and children enjoy their toys,
while we go to visit your tomb,
and cry near your head.

We miss you,
in the first Eid,
while you are far away from us,
we will not say farewell,
but we will meet there soon,
to celebrate our Eid.

GAZA – JUST FOUR LETTERS

Just four letters,
written with the water of gold,
like the stars in the sky,
like a full moon.

Gaza has four letters,
our souls are ready for you,
our blood so cheap,
our children are your soldiers.

Just four letters,
your enemies know you,
it is difficult to pass,
so hard to conquer,
so steadfast and patient.

Just four letters,
your enemies know your men,
so hard to beat,
so furious to the fight,
very strong men.

Just four letters,
your enemies know you well,
impossible to surrender,
unacceptable to raise the white flag,
stubborn to forget our rights.

Just four letters,
make the soldiers dream of nightmares,
dreams with ghosts,
unable to deceive people,
unable to make progress.

Just four letters,
soldiers unable to leave tanks,
or show their heads,
their skulls on the borders,
their flesh is everywhere.

Just four letters,
your people grind the sand,
carve in the rocks,
drink the water of sea,
dig the earth for food.

Gaza… just four letters,
and it will stand forever.

IT WILL NEVER BE BROKEN

Gaza will stand,
it will never be broken,
they have said many years,
Gaza is the tomb of the invaders,
none of invaders will last long,
it is like a volcano,
throws its lava outside its walls,
more hot than any hell,
burns the conquerors,
grinds their bones,
hangs their skulls on the borders,
swallows their bodies in the sea.

Gaza will stand,
it will never be broken,
series of attacks,
different kinds of battles,
various lethal weapons,
inhumane armies,
comprehensive destruction,
the blind world collaborates.

Gaza will stand,
it will never be broken,
convoys of martyrs,
countless number of wounded,
thousands of prisoners,
dozens of orphans,

hundreds of disabled,
so many widows,
unlimited types of crises.

Gaza will stand,
it will never be broken,
the blood of martyrs,
the pain of many wounded,
the loss of sons and daughters,
the screaming of many prisoners,
the crying of mothers,
and the mourning of fathers,
the broken hearts of widows,
and the compassion of orphans,
destruction of homes.

Forever, Gaza will stand,
it will never be broken.

SOME GLASSES OF WHISKEY

Since I was born,
they used to attack me,
they raped me in the day,
and stole me in the night,
they plotted to kill me,
my parents were killed,
my sisters abandoned me.

They were the whores,
who sold their dignity and rights,
they were like the blind,
but with eyes to witness,
their crimes against me.

There ... in that night bar,
they conspired with the robbers,
after having some glasses of Whiskey,
and after the red nights,
on that luxurious bed,
they signed the documents,
Gaza must be occupied,
and the story started,
the robbers came to the land,
stole the blessings,
as promised,
the land of milk and honey,
they killed the residents,

destroyed their homes,
extinguished the culture,
required people to leave their homeland,
spread the terror and fear.

A day after a long night,
Gaza was occupied,
where is an occupation,
there will be resistance,
but the robbers were armed,
supported by the boss,
the number of martyrs,
more than the year of my birthday,
the wounded people are limitless,
the destroyed homes are everywhere,
the massacres are massive,
the robbers are so proud,
the more you kill,
the more you will honor.

Then war after war,
and the Palestinians wait,
for the day of their freedom.

HOW CAN I FORGET YOU?!

Each dawn you come to my mind,
every hour of the day,
your image ticks the o'clock,
with every knock on the door,
I imagine you are returning.

The smell of your body,
comes through your clothes,
with every drop of water,
your voice passes through my ears,
with every wave of the sea,
I remember our days,
with every long night,
I feel your warmth,
put my hand on your pillow,
with every drop of tears,
I feel you.

How can I forget you?!,
you are alive there,
Await my coming to you,

How can I forget you?!,
while your photos are on every wall of our home,
how can I forget you?!,
you left three children to me,
they look like you,

have the same smell,

and the same eyes,
which I see you through.

How can I forget you?!,
while they ask about you,
is our father there in Paradise?!,
we want go there to join him.

How can I forget you?!
especially every Thursday,
I visit your tomb,
let you listen to my prayers,
and my heart beats for you,
you are my martyred husband,
How can I forget you?!.

"How Can We Forget?"
A lot of memories in our minds,
many events curved in history,
the ancestors narrate the generations,
about the suffering and pain.

When they were forced to leave,
their homes, animals and farms,
you see the tears in their eyes,
and the sorrow of their faces.

The heart is aching with pain,
they dream to go back,
and reside again in their villages,
they say "Do not ever give up",
they surrender the keys to the young,

to carve the homeland in the hearts,
they keep the documents safe,

because one day we will go back,
the atrocities against our parents,
who immigrated when they were young,
suffer the hunger and pain,
live in tents with no food,
some died because of sickness,
lack of medicine and awareness,
raped the women in prisons,
jailed the old youth with torture.

How can we forget?,
the war against the Palestinians,
the massacres in Lebanon,
Sabra and Shatela atrocities are examples,
witness their savage crimes.

How can we forget?,
the killing of our parents,
the torture of the prisoners,
the blood of our martyrs,
the injuries of the wounded,
the pain and suffering of the neighbors.

How can we forget?!,
the tears of the mothers,
the loss of our families,
the killing of our children,
destruction of our bodies,
the mourning of the relatives,
the screaming of the children.

AHMED MIQDAD

How can we forget?!,
the demolished homes,
the trees cut down,

the burning of our land,
the many displaced families,
the destruction of so many homes.

How can we forget?!,
the explosions of the bombs,
the sounds of blasts,
the heavy explosives,
the prohibited rockets,
the destructive weapons.

How can we forget?!,
the darkness of the nights,
the horror of our mothers,
the terrorism of our children,
the fear of our parents,
How can we forget?!.

JERUSALEM

My heart is burning,
it is torn into pieces,
my bones are boiling,
like the fire of the hell,
to burn all aggressors,
who attack you every day,
kill your residents,
I am gone from you,
cannot do anything,
or take any action.

The previous times made you,
as a stubble for horses,
no more calls out from minarets,
they devastated you,
made you a place for rubbish.

They intend to capture you,
keep you away from us,
put checkpoints and terminals,
we see your bright dome in newspapers,
the settlers step on your holy land,
with armed guards,
spread impurity over your sand,
they deprive Palestinians,
of praying inside you.

AHMED MIQDAD

They burn my heart,
when they burnt you,
they plan to destroy you,

they dig tunnels under you,
but you will be stronger,
be patient and conquer them.

I cannot reach you,
I have to be sixty,
to get a permission to pass,
but you will be always,
in my sincere prayers,
ask Allah to protect you.

MY PRIDE

My pride….,
You are so beautiful,
a tall lady like the map,
that has different geographical colors,
includes desserts, seas,
mountains, coasts, and hills.

You are my pride,
slim like the borders,
you are so soft,
like the sand of the coast,
with blue eyes,
like the water of the sea,
during a pure sky,
crowed with stars,
you are so glamorous,
when your image comes up,
on the pages of the waves,
you are shining,
like the golden minarets of the mosques,
especially the yellow dome.

Away there ….,
look at you every morning,
but cannot reach you,
it is enough to raise my hand,
towards your golden necklace.

AHMED MIQDAD

In my heart,
your garden grows ,
full of trees bearing fruit,
oranges like yellow jewels,
olive trees with a unique oil,
bright like the green diamonds.

You are my pride,
one day time will come,
and we will celebrate,
our dowry will be "Freedom",
the witnesses will be your people,
the martyrs will be,
the stars of the celebration,
convoys and convoys of martyrs,
look at you in ecstasy,
their blood is your fragrant,
spread everywhere all over the place,
light the candles with their blood,
widows, wounded,
orphans and prisoners,
will be the audience,
you will be the husband of widows,
the mother of the orphans,
the healing of wounded,
the stage will be,
between the demolished homes,
and above the rubble and debris.

You are my pride….,
we will celebrate together,
when you get your freedom.

AHMED MIQDAD

MY SON... THEY KILLED YOU

The day comes knock on the door,
with a hope it will be peaceful,
during the claimed truce,
instead of birds singing,
the sky was full of drones,
like black birds.

He went to play,
in the near playground,
the drone attacked him and his mates,
while they were playing football,
his ball came back with blood,
but he didn't come back home,
he travelled away without farewell,
met him in the hospital,
with his head cut and a broken body,
they killed my son,
they burnt my heart.

Remember the diaries of my son,
he used to kiss my hand,
when he comes back from school,
shows the good marks,
and the appreciation of his teachers,
still check the notebooks,
smell his bag and clothes,
kept some of his blood,

AHMED MIQDAD

on a piece of cloth,

I used to visit his tomb,
read some prayers,
while my tears are falling,
speak with him quietly,
say, "I love you".

He lives in my mind,
his face is on my mirror,
his scent is everywhere in our the home,
I imagine, he plays near me,
confused between him and his brother,
called his brother by his name.

Notice the fire,
in his mother's eyes,
which will burn your killer,
who killed you with the drone,
break you into small pieces.
The sorrow of his brother,
who lost a brother and a friend.

My sympathy in this life,
we will meet there one day,
without killing or drones,
live peacefully in heaven,
and Almighty will burn them,
as they burnt our hearts.

A LEG OR A HEART?

The smell of blood is everywhere,
it covers my body with the smell,
the red color waters the clothes and sand,
my old white jacket is now red,
the deep wounds kill me inside,
the unbearable pain has me faint,
the cut leg is bleeding continuously,
no paramedics or bandages,
unable to move from that place.

Near the destroyed home,
far away from people,
rubble spread over my body,
my family are all dead,
gaze to my children,
then fainted,
woke up again.
my wife is in the other side,
then lost my awareness.

Unable to help myself,
or check my dead family,
I felt so cold,
my body loses blood,
so difficult to take the breath,
so dizzy and sleepy,
like a mountain over my eyelashes,

none sees us under the debris.

I was in a tomb,
but I was alive,
wait the moment of death,
sun rays passes through a small hole,
then sun went far away,
the darkness attacked the place,
I cannot see my family,
then stay quiet awaiting death,
it was a wish,
to go there with them.

A red siren lit the hole,
hear a voice screaming,
"Is there any alive?",
"Is there any alive?"
I cannot reply at him,
he was about to leave,
but I loudly shouted " Yes, help",
he returned and put the torch in the hole,
he saw me and said be calm,
he digs to remove the rubble.

I found myself laying on the hospital bed,
shall you treat my lost leg?
or shall you cure my broken heart for losing my family?
I can live without a leg or two,
but I cannot live without a heart.

PLEASE, DON'T COME

You are so welcomed guest,
you bring blessings with you,
you are the reason for flowers,
and the life to plants,
you help earth to cover,
the sand with green cover.

But for Gazans,
you are not welcomed at all,
especially this time,
your rain will submerge,
our demolished homes,
your winds will eradicate,
our soft tents,
your thunder will crash so loud,
it will remind us of war,
sounds of bombs and explosions,
our children will be afraid,
Please, do not come.

Our homes are demolished,
our clothes are under the debris,
the covers and mats are mixed with blood,
our tents cannot protect you,
Please, do not come.

We want build our homes,

mend our broken parts,

we need heavy clothes,
save the children from your cold.

Please, come next year,
wash the black days away,
clean our hearts,
from the sadness,
remove the wounds,
which were deeply carved into our bodies,
pour your water,
wash the blood from streets,
spread peace and a new born life,
Please, do not come now.

THE APARTEID WALL WILL FALL

I miss my cup of coffee,
during the morning,
there on the white table,
near that big wall,
which deprived Palestinians,
of visits to their relatives.

There, behind the wall,
which bans the mother,
from meeting her daughter,
from the near village,
which stole our lands,
kill our olive trees,
planted years ago.

That savage wall,
which cut the relatives,
destroy the relations,
and cut the hearts.

I miss visiting my land,
miss seeing my fruitful trees,
and miss the simple dish,
under the orange tree,
which was planted by my parents.

The settlers stole the land,

and kicked us off,

with the support of the soldiers,
bulldozers eliminate homes and trees,
while we have no choice,
we have our faith and axes,
against armed settlers,
but they will not steal our will.

We will return,
the wall will be removed,
and our willing will win,
while the wall is falling.

We will win,
with deep faith and hope,
the land will come back,
and the right will come back,
to the real and true owners,
the apartheid wall will fall.

GAZA THE BIG PRISON

Gaza is a historical legend,
or is it a sacred miracle,
it stands in front of us,
the forth army in the world,
hanging their skulls,
on the wires of the borders,
turn their tanks into tombs,
bury the barbarian invaders,
near the coast of the sea.

All the world is against you,
You are planning to get rid of us,
drawing strategies and tactics,
all were in vain,
close the borders in front of,
your wounded and needy,
the siege is all around,
apparent enemy is there,
and a silent one is here.

They want to kill you, Gaza,
with their Siege imposed on the sea,
only a few miles to fish,
shoot the boats and the fishermen,
confiscate their rusty ships,
we are unable to get out,
you have taken our rights,
to travel,

to trade,
to study,
even to live.

But we will never surrender,
though our hearts are aching,
our brothers there,
close our borders,
to obey their big boss,
they left us to die,
no medicine,
no food,
no rights as humans,
all sides are bound,
thousands are waiting to travel,
wounded people are aching,
waiting for their chance to leave,
with hope to get treatment,
to their deep wounds,
tears in the eyes of relatives,
wish they could,
meet each other out there.

Years and years of killing,
war and so many atrocities,
is it the time?!,
to get our freedom,
to live like all humans,
but shame on you,
my unfair world,
you are the reason,
they let us die each moment,
if people died once,

we die by the thousands,

and yet you are silent.

We will be patient,
never giving up,
and we will live in our prison,
inside my bleeding Gaza,
we will provide for it,
with our red blindness,
and you will conquer,
all your enemies.

All gates are closed,
but don't forget the gates of heaven, there
it will not return back a knocker,
let's knock at the gates of justice,
to break our big prison down.

AHMED MIQDAD

THE KEY

The key is in his hand,
tears are in his eyes,
there is hope that resides in his heart,
the ownership papers are in an old box,
it is rusty with a lock,
under the bed of my ancestors,
they have strong faith,
we will return,
and the door of the stolen house,
is waiting for our return.
The grape trees on the farm,
want to give its fruit.

The village is so sad,
like a raped girl,
Zionists forced our people to leave,
stole their homes and lands,
killed many Palestinians,
blood now irrigates the fields,
it has witnessed the crimes,
of the Israeli occupation.

The mosque in the village,
abandoned without prayers,
turned into a Jewish school,
teaching the instructions and practices,
of hatred and killing,
against the innocent Palestinians.

The village will have its revenge,
they will sink in its river,
thrown from the highest mountains,
the land will be returned,
and it will show happiness,
of being back among its owners.

A NIGHT OF AUTUMN

Winds blow strongly,
the leaves flying everywhere,
leave the branches of trees,
the trees no longer have a green shelter,
the clouds have gathered together,
covering the blue sky,
the earth is bare,
no home or shelter like the tree,
in the autumn semester.

The home was demolished,
the soft bed was broken,
the toys of the children were buried,
and tears were shed like rain,
stay inside this cloth tent,
make it strong in the earth,
tied cords in the earth,
to buffer the bitter winds,
with hope that the earth will protect us,
and the sky that holds the rain,
light the fire inside the tent,
gather the children around us,
that they might feel the warmth,
bake some bread to eat,
boil milk for the youngest,
then let them sleep.

While their tiny hearts are beating,

the sky disgorges its' rain,
the winds are so severe,
the earth is flooded,
no one is outside,
except the barking dogs,
under the rubble of homes nearby,
so afraid of the water and the winds,
continually checking on the children,
to ensure the tent is still strong.

After mid-night,
flooding creeps into the tent,
how can I evacuate the children?!,
where can I evacuate them to?!,
shall I put them under the fallen homes?!,
shall I move them under the rubble of my home,
beside the homeless dogs?!,
the cords were cut off,
the sky poured down water,
the earth left us,
the tent flew away.

But the choice was,
stay with the dogs under the rubble,
they might have more mercy,
than some of our mankind.

THE RED PILLOW

The night covered the light,
silence came so quickly,
the streets are empty,
the darkness kills the candles.

With every explosion,
the voices of the screaming,
people escape from the hell,
we were obliged to taste,
not with our tongues,
but with our hearts.

The fear stills my heartbeat,
and the rockets kill the bodies,
you are ready to sacrifice,
and to be split into pieces,
to keep the children safe,
your children are not any better,
than those that were killed,
and buried under the rubble,
as their smell came out,
but it is the paternity,
to feel afraid for your children,
and it is not easy to see,
your children leave you,
without saying farewell.

During that dark night,
sleeping with the whole family,

and the fear pours into our hearts,
pretending to be strong,
in front of the children,
to make them a little stronger,
I sleep near the children,
on the same white pillow,
so tired of bombs all the day,
and from big explosions through the night.

There was a close attack,
but none cared about,
then felt the pillow is wet,
it is so dark without a light,
I was in a sea,
but a sea of my son's blood,
when I put my head on the pillow,
I dream that I sink deeply,
inside that dark ocean,
wait until the day appears,
to live the nightmare truly,
as I found myself covered,
with the blood of my son,
when the white pillow,
became a red one.

THE ROBBERS

This chaotic world,
countries are engaged in their own interests,
strong counties control the weak,
the robbers utilized the time,
they robbed Palestine,
stole the holy land,
killed the residents,
forced the rest to immigrate,
they took the important areas,
cut the trees,
demolished Palestinian homes,
stole the culture,
changed the name of streets,
removed the Palestinian tombs.

They are the robbers,
who shoot our children,
let mothers cry,
make parents bury their sons,
arrest our youth and put them in prisons,
destroy the homes above the innocents,
and cause wives to mourn their husbands.

They are the robbers,
they stole our happiness,
terrorized the Palestinian families,
deflower our virgin Palestine,
rob the joy of our life,

took our legal rights.

They are the robbers,
and we are the owner.

THE SKY OF GAZA IS RAINING

The sky of Gaza is raining,
the sky is blue,
but there are clouds of smokes,
full of drones,
F-16s and helicopters,
winds blow from the explosions,
with each blast a new storm,
earthquakes shake our homes,
because of those lethal bombs.

It is summer and the sky is raining,
so strange,
it rains missiles and bombs,
explosives and bullets,
it rains dogs and cats.

Be safe and be secure,
stay away from windows,
the broken glass is flying,
the debris of bodies on the walls,
corpses are in the streets,
flood of red blood,
stay close to your kids,
to make sure we die all together,
and no one left who feels sad for the other,
no one left to mourn others.

The strong missiles will reach you,
turn your soft body into pieces,

burn your bones,
distort your features.

My little birds are so afraid,
they are in their nest,
making slight sounds,
with every sound of the explosions,
my white doves don't fly,
there is no empty space to fly,
the black birds hover and will attack,
kids cling so tight to their mothers.

The screaming of the kids,
breaks the silence,
darkness is everywhere,
my lovely candle gives some light,
so frightened from the attacks,
and from the candle while burning,
the bright light comes from outside,
the bombs are like thunders,
with a panicked red light,
the smell of death comes,
it knocks on the doors.

Please! Don't knock my door,
I'm a father with three small kids,
it is too early to take us,
we love life,
we have dreams to live,
we are like butterflies,
falling on the beautiful scenes,
go out of my city,
it is full of children,
women, innocent men,
don't deprive us of life,

our father is a good man,
with a white heart and kind manners,
we want to stay together,
like other children worldwide.

I appeal to you,
move the clouds, drones,
bombs and explosives,
we hope the sky will rain,
hope and peace,
freedom and welfare,
replace our bad memories,
with sweet dreams

WE WILL NEVER SURRENDER

We will never surrender,
If we strive for victory ,
We will grind the sand to eat,
If we are thirsty,
We will drink the sea water,
If we are homeless,
We will make the earth our beds,
And the sky our blanket,
If all doors are closed,
We will knock on the door of the sky,
If all the trees are cut,
We will plant more and more and more,
If we lose our babies,
We will give birth to thousands more,
We will never surrender,
In spite of the thousands of martyrs,
And the pain of our prisoners' mothers,
The tears of our widows,
The loss of our limbs,
The cries of our wounded,
The pieces of broken bodies,
The rubble of our homes,
The crying of our orphans,
The corpses of our dead bodies,
The sounds of your warplanes,
The sounds of your bombs,
The fear of our children,
We will never surrender,

Although you are the knife,
And we are the flesh,
You are the killer ,
And we are the murdered,
You are the kidnapper,
And we are the hostages,
You are the oppressor,
And we are the oppressed,
You are the occupier,
And we are the occupied,
You are the strong because of your weapons,
And we are the strong because of our faith,
You are the rock,
And we are the drops,
Drop, drop, drop,
The rock may crack,
But we will never surrender.

WAITING FOR THE SHIP

The sun is sinking behind the sea,
the horizon is so glamorous,
the sea is quiet,
sitting near the beach,
counting wave after wave,
waiting for the ship of hope,
of peace, love, and freedom.

Many people on the beach,
looking for the sunshine,
wishing a new day would come,
after paying the price,
thousands of martyrs,
the screaming of widows,
the pains of the wounded,
mourning of sons and daughters,
loss of limbs,
the killing of our children,
especially as this beach witnesses,
the crimes of the Israelis.

Wait day after day,
people come and go,
years are passing,
while I am waiting,
watching ship after ship,
waiting for my ship to come.

An old man once told me,
we have waited a long time,
as our fathers before us,
they died and we will follow,
but we will keep waiting,
one day that ship we waited for,
will come to the beach,
the generations will witness,
as the freedom rises,
like the sun in summer,
and like the fourteenth night moon.

WE WILL SMILE

We will smile,
although we lost our beloved,
we lost our husbands,
lost our wives under debris.

We will smile,
though you stole our children,
the wounds are so deep,
the hearts are so weak.

We will smile,
from the destroyed homes,
from our tents,
and from every hospital bed.

We will smile,
in spite of the mourning for whole families,
the martyrdom of martyrs,
the pains of wounded,
the loss of body parts,
the pieces of the shredded bodies,
the homeless families.

We will smile,
though you kill our children,
you make our blood,
like a river in the streets,
you eradicate our hearts,
though our bodies are still alive,

you split us apart,
and shred bodies litter.

We will smile,
while our hearts are bleeding,
with a pain so intense,
the bitterness of life,
the parents' visit to the tombs,
you can take everything,
except the smiles on our faces,
So, we will smile.

GAZA WILL STAND UP AGAIN

It is so clear,
the wound is so deep,
the loss is eminent,
the tears have not dried yet,
the heart is still bleeding,
the smell of blood is everywhere,
the remains of destruction,
are so apparent.

We lost relatives and friends,
lost children and families,
the number is too big,
a lot of martyrs passed away,
thousands of wounded,
suffer the pain of their wounds,
from one hospital to another,
thousands of demolished homes,
so, thousands of homeless families,
lack of medicine and care,
shortage of power and water,
besieged for years.

The world is biased,
or it is blind,
war after war,
without condemnation,
but we will stand up again,
we will deliver babies,
we will name them,

with the names of martyrs,
we will heal our deep wounds.

We will stand up again,
we will rebuild our demolished homes,
and plant more trees,
we will grind the sand to eat if we have to,
and we will dig up rocks to drink,
we will get up from the sand,
we will remove the tears,
and draw the smiles instead,
together, a hand within a hand,
we will stand up again.

WHO AM I?!

Who Am I?!
I am the victim,
and you are my murderer,
by your silence,
and your blind eyes,
by your support to the aggressor,
and your blame to the oppressed.

Who Am I?!,
I am the martyr,
and you are my killer,
you killed me savagely,
with your bombs and explosives,
you killed me with your weapons,
under the rubble of my home.

Who Am I?!,
I am the occupied,
and you are my occupier,
you forced my parents,
to leave their lands,
you stole that land,
and cut down the trees,
you shed so much blood,
kill the innocents,
jail the resistant,
destroy the homes,
and commit many inhumane atrocities.

Who am I?!,
I am the wounded,
and you are my wound,
you are the lethal pain,
you are the sour wound,
and you are the deep crack.

Who am I?!,
I am the widow,
you took my husband,
with your destructive wars,
and your wrathful behaviors,
you made the heart cry,
and the eyes flood with tears,
you are the sadness,
that resides in our hearts.

Who am I?!
I am the homeless,
and you are the reason,
you are the rockets that destroy,
you are the bombs that demolish,
you are the missiles that cut,
the heads and body parts,
you are the siege that deprives.

Who am I?!,
I am the strong by my faith,
and you are the weak by your weapons,
I am the strong by my sons,
and you are the weak by your mercenaries,
I am the strong by my ownership,
and you are the weak by your occupation.

Who am I?!,
I am the orphan,
and you killed my parents,
my sons, and my family,
you stole the smile from my face,
you killed happiness in my life,
you changed my sweet dreams to nightmares,
you took my soul,
while I am still alive.

Who am I?,
I am Palestine.
And you are the occupation.
I am Palestine,
And you are Israhell.

WOUNDED GAZA

Many dark nights,
a lot of pale days,
years full of sufferings,
war after war,
and the future more severe,
years of siege,
countless crises,
like the cluster of grapes.

Don't know how to start,
power or water,
unemployment or poverty,
terminals or check points,
travel or fuel.
people are so patient,
in spite of it all,
but how long will this last?!.

Gaza is surrounded,
by occupiers and betrayers,
sea from the west,
mixed with blood,
coast lined with shredded bodies,
but it is the only friendly place,
to smell freedom,
and wait for the victory,
count the waves with hope,
wave after wave,
waiting for the ship of freedom,

to come to the beach.

Occupiers deprive Gazans,
and take away their right to live,
or think more than healing wounds,
war after war,
more people killed,
unlimited demolished homes,
big numbers of martyrs,
all are wounded,
if not physically,
it will be psychologically,
homeless are countless,
full of streets and schools.

This unfair world,
makes the murderer a victim,
and the victim becomes a criminal,
stolen the lands and the rights.

Gaza is so wounded,
took the whole land,
give us the smallest part,
and we want to take it,
Gaza has been bleeding for so long,
years are a witness to them all,
lands blended with blood,
trees were cut,
innocents were punished,
no one moves.

Gaza is wounded,
the world is sleeping,
have no business with Gaza,
no humanity at all,

years and years of suffering,
officials are dead for Gaza,
alive to serve the occupiers.

We are so deceived,
United Nations or International Security Council,
they are servants for the occupiers,
while we are dying in Gaza,
massive and savage killing of Gazans,
as defending oneself,
while a group resists the occupiers,
it is a great crime,
and they condemn us,
shame on such a blind world.

We are humans,
looking for human rights,
we love life and hate killing,
but no fairness in this world,
and Gaza is still wounded.

THE WALKING DEAD

The souls are still inside their bodies,
the blood pumps through their hearts,
they are walking in the streets,
have you seen them?!.

The Dead are walking on their feet,
I have seen so many of them,
or maybe you should say all Gazans are dead,
some have lost their souls,
and others are just waiting around.

Don't be sad for the ones that have gone,
be sad for the ones who are still alive,
those that have to stay,
inside the big cage,
some went to live in the wide heaven,
and the rest are encountering their destiny,
living with fear and terror,
every second of the day,
facing the nightmares during the night,
with dreams of blood and pain,
remembering the atrocities,
of the murdered parents and families,
imagine the loss of so many children,
living the life of orphans,
see the plotting of our enemies,
every morning and evening.

At least, the dead will not,
hear the sounds of bombs,

see the planes hover,
or the remains of bodies on the pavement,
they will not taste,
the meaning of fear,
the emotions of loss,
and the pain of the wounded,
but the walking dead,
feel everything that occurs,
lives the crises daily,
no power for long hours,
salty water like the sea,
shortage of fuel,
the killing siege,
and half-paid salaries,
this ugly occupation,
and the losses of our beloved,
farewell to our relatives,
hello to our closed borders,
welcome to the big prison,
massive unemployment,
nothing but a frozen life,
how can we bear this?!.

We are the walking dead,
living inside our cage,
inside the broken Gaza,
we will never give up,
in spite of this lethal crises,
we don't wait for food,
or supplies and humanitarian aid,
but we are waiting,
for freedom and peace.